THE BOTTOM LINE

Jack Hirschman

Curbstone Press

The author wishes to thank the following journals in which some of these poems first appeared: *Alcatraz, Bachy, Compages, Dalmo'ma Anthology, Haight-Ashbury Literary Journal, Left Curve, Lovelights, North Beach Magazine, Oboe, Oro Madre, Peace or Perish Anthology, The People's Tribune, Poet News, Poetry San Francisco* and *Struggle.* Some are reprinted from the chapbooks, *Kallatumba* (Ruddy Duck Press) and *The Necessary Is* (Fishy Afoot Press).

First Edition
Printed in the United States at Curbstone Press

This publication was supported in part by The Connecticut Commission on the Arts, a State agency whose funds are recommended by the Governor and appropriated by the State Legislature, and in part by the contributions of numerous individuals.

Cover design by Stone Graphics
Cover photograph by John Murao

LC Number: 87-73443
ISBN: 0-915306-73-5

distributed by
THE TALMAN COMPANY
150 Fifth Avenue
New York, NY 10011

CURBSTONE PRESS
321 Jackson Street, Willimantic, CT 06226

For Our Gentle Comrades

TABLE OF CONTENTS

THE BOTTOM LINE

THE CALL FOR THE LOVE OF THE PEOPLE

The dead alive, the small children,
the illiterate
yes as a unanimous verb
yes the soul of the people's arts,
tell of the fetuses of stones
waiting for the birth of revolution
within the womb continuum,
how the trees are sick of being locked
in corporate forests,
and how you, my love
my sex my tenderness,
are weary of the price
nailed like a snake to your inner spine,
dollarsign of thingdom,
sign that divides the idea
into factions of penniless backbite
so that unity is shut up
in a mouth that used to be singing
and now merely mumbles in time.

Look, because a body is buried or
cremated or vanishes
doesn't mean it ceases seeding,
doesn't mean it ceases growing
the liberation tree.
The tattered kids left motherless
when those ten beautiful fingers
of Guatemala were beheaded
have to do with your pen, your brush,
your dance, your xylophony.
There are eyes that never have seen
a book or a pen,
planted on top of a mouth
that is wandering in a desert
starving for a thousand years,

9

and they literally are
speaking you this
from the orbs of their anguish;
it's they who are behind
the telepathy of hope
which antidotes
the injection of rumpling black leather
and the poisonous neon
fascism's dosed you with.

There is no distance between us
and the heroic cry of the spark
of the child burned
forever to be flaming.
O fetus that can look forward
to being nothing
but the awful emulation
of your mother's belly – quick, comrades
we must destroy those capitalist dogs!
Then you, my thin bone, my nomad brother,
my sequoyah in this wilderness of wounds,
shall read these words tear by tear
and I shall taste the courageous
syllabary of your song.

VLADIMIR MAYAKOVSKY

You, thunderer and swirl of
       the flag of blood and roses,
kneader of the bread of poem,
deathless comrade of dithyramb
     and liberty,
you whose suicided life
     I carry as a forge,
who first strode the street
     of this century,
ai, you were the first
singing through the slum of trash
and the molecules chained
to a thousand yesterdays,
wiper of the gravy of history
from the mouth of obese lies,
servant of revolution,
you who, among men, stormed
the pallid lips of neutrality
and apathy,
not as a stud of craven doom,
not as *semblable*
but as a thrust and momentum
of mass and energy
announcing the towering totems
of humanity freed from the hut,
you russian more american
than english,
you sabbath-destroyer
and leveller of twirpery
and religious doubletalk,
I have plucked the bullet
so many times from your brain
I could feed a hundred
armed struggles with your dream.

11

SELF-PORTRAIT

Sitting on a
factory-wall ledge
waiting for a bus at night,
the sense of my jacket on me,
the feel of my face, american, man,
it's cold, lighting a cigaret,
feeling my brow
not with my hand
but feeling it, the lines
in it, wind-furrowed
and everyday,
relative to, after all,
the wheels rolling by,
the factory,
nights like this one
helping a friend
or tumbled out of the hair
of hooch, how many
like myself, the dark car
passing by, hey yo,
the booming double
Nielson freight, hey
yo, full face
way up there
in a dark outskirt, equal.

THE CHINESE WOMEN

The Chinese women
move in the hotel corridors
in their pyjamas,
appearing from around a corner
or out of a door
like ether. They keep
the hotel corridors neat
and tidy simply by walking
up and down, sharing
a word, then disappearing
into a room to scrub
some greens or put
a bowl of rice before
a child. Even the raunchy
and noisy street people
in the hotel are stilled
by these women. You
wouldn't know the thunder
of a needle hitting a vein
from the whisper of cockroaches
with such creatures around.
We come from families
and are estranged from our own
blood in our own bloody
fucking hustle of a land.
They don't even speak our tongue
yet make space a life
called home and work, like
way back then. They
are like the insides of pillows
in a world that no longer sleeps.
They know how to brown all food
so that it's good to eat.

13

THE PORTRAIT

You were always water to me,
this vessel, this boat
of a body full of
syllables - from you who
accidently in the sense
of chance, in the French
sense of *hasard*, gave
me your life to care for,
a life I care for,
fashion from its immense stillness
the noise of propaganda,
this madness but clear sailing
of thirst for your repose:

a love in many places
forming a chin,
many lenses forming a pair
of eyes,
many forms of hair forming
a form of hair,
whose silence makes others speak,
who exist outside of my
hearing you -

    I am sick of hearing a world
call you shit
call you bad
call you weird
call you devil
call you god.

I live with you eternally; -
when I see face inside
my face, it is yours;
when I smash the barriers
of usury and vice,
of all the mechanisms of
capital and the inventions
of steel used to defend them,
when I fill with comrades
and streets, wires and volts
of religious creeds,
it is you who see me through
the struggle to feel
your form again,

face, communist face,
that never will I sell
to the machinery of woe,
face I will go to my grave with,
simple face, face of nature,
style of a century artificed
and complex,
whose journey is to face
the face of pure
confrontation within,
to be destroyed into poem
again and again by it,
to be reborn with the millions
of other red faces,
face of my handsweat,
face I defend against
the violence of time
of history kissed
in prisons of thighs,
in prosodies of wires of diplomacies,
face which multiplies

15

from the one,
from the bipolar forms
of bridgings and abdominal cries,
face of chance
I have rendered
eternally revolutionary,
turning from everything
backward, revisionist,
merely historical,
to keep me,
no matter how
many changes

    of music, of
    records,
    of lovers,
    of streetcars,
    of conversions to
        religions
    of whirligig lies,

read with you
as a breath
for which there is
no breathing but everything
        fills with lung,
no movement but everything
        is in motion,

and what it names
is the stillness,
the silence,
from which will emerge

the minutiae and grandiosity
of these dialects
of the tribe
it purifies

with every thought
of its resolution
and its revolution
as the word.

THE GRAFFITI

The scraped Chinatown wall
still has bits of
the Mayday poster on it.

It is like an abstract
painting now
and my senses are stirred
with sorrow and delight,
so momentary
and atomized are they:

the transient hotel
looks up at the skyscraper,
the skyscraper looks down
at the transient hotel.

In the window of the latter
a man is smoking
a cigaret.
In the windows of the skyscraper
I can see nothing.

I didn't even realize it
when suddenly there were
only the crumbs of nature
and when I tried to write
of the sea
or thunder-rolls
and lightning flashing after,
when I tried seeing the sun
on the eagle's wings
with the brave eyes
of a simpler poetry,
a military music intervened
like an arm and a hand

18

tearing the scene from my heart
like that Mayday poster.

How sad
to be this moment
for beauty
so smithereened.

Mine is not yours and yours
is not another's and
so on till the end of our breaths, yet
here, there, and elsewhere
we are the cries of graffiti
prouder than the stories
told by robots

and even in the gutter-ruts
and the striations made
by fool-fingers and weatherlash
of wind

the hieroglyphs of our seasons
can be read.

A CIAO WITH A NEIGHBORHOOD AROUND IT

A ciao with a neighborhood
around it.
I looked from the window,
saw the horse and wagon
and the vegetable man
and the women coming out
in their thin cotton
housedresses.

To my right, in the next house,
Junior Monaco, my friend.
To my left, in the next house,
Mestrop Sahagian, my friend.
Behind me, in the rear flat,
Stanley Wrubel, my friend.

Before me, the street,
the vegetable man, the shitplopping
horse, the chalkmarks of potsy,
the johnnypump, the sewers –
I could hit two and a half sewers –
yesterday's rain dirty along
the curb,

20

a car passing, then another
with a California plate black
and gold and written across
the numbers in red: Hitler will
commit suicide, the war will end,
the world will become cars, but you will
grow up and live in a little village
in San Francisco and walk and
hear ciao, and know the horse and horseshit
and the vegetable man and the
women in their thin cotton dresses.
Old friends.

MOTHER

We are not in this world
a long time ago
it happened it was over:
the world the war the world war.
I took you by the hand
through it,
tiniest hand, tiniest star.
You didn't move then
I was dead, then you were dead.
In the open mouth of grief
there is a candle.

I am not with my breath,
I am the slow peeling away
of the skin
and all that all the deaths
I've seen registers
in my eyes.
I have been a laughing tree
beside a stove
of honeyed bananas,
I have been a silver fox
and the elegance of heels,
I have been what has
brought you down
and the words you look up,
I have been the spit-upon
and the ganged,
the slain and the invincible,
the bitch of moons,
the whiplash of compassion
behind the drug of sluts,
the red thread that
liberates all convicts,
the thimble that balances

your jiggers,
the kalimba that wraps
your nightmares in lullabies,
the power of birth
when a child dies.

We are not in this world
a long time ago
it happened it was over:
the world the war the world war.
I took you by the hand
through it,
tiniest hand, tiniest star.
Why should I weep now now
that you have entered the darkness?
Many like me are around you.
Our ether is without end.
Should we never speak again,
you shall write our conversation.
Should my voice fall short of your heart
(but that is impossible,
you're still such a child,
I'm weeping at a window),
other voices will lift mine
and carry it to the center
of your breathing.

O my beloved, when you burst into flames,
when your bones were blistered,
at those precise moments,
who drove the seeds in a rapid
torrent of thighs and targeted
the yearning eggs with glory?
When you grew like a primer
into a text of rage
at all the injustice of this
profiteering hell,

when your mind was broken,
when your sex was split
like Korea, Vietnam,
like the North and South,
when poisons came with pleasure
and the antidote was dead,
who cut through the air
as if wringing a chicken's neck?
Who tore the feathers and flung them
to cushion your fall?

I am the creature who runs through the streets
screaming your name against the mockery,
I am the sleep of the suicide
and the cataract of immemorial hair,
I am the attack of liberty on the hard of heart
and the poem on the hard of hearing.
The solitude, the grace, the smile
that returns your smile
from the depths of the biology
of a labor and joy
only the heartbeats of the dithyramb approach,
only the soul thrums of the cosmos define.

We are not in this world
a long time ago
it happened it was over:
the world the war the world war.
I took you by the hand
through it,
tiniest hand, tiniest star.

TWILIGHT

The swiftly low
moving San Francisco
fog passing thru
the steeple
like people
in a hurry
to the grey furrier.

ONE NIGHT

One night, many North Beach years ago,
after a reading at the old Coffee Gallery,
drunk, I found myself in my single bed
at the old New Riviera hotel
making love to a young woman.
She was fair and lithe and craving
and I was lonely and poet-stung.
After love she slept in my arms.
It was then I saw her body's marks, the extensive
track record of her race
and rose and sat and wrote
a dozen little love poems
to her beauty and despair,
and all you can imagine as she slept.
She was gone by morning
but I saw her two weeks later
on one of the Columbus Day floats
that passed down Stockton by the Park.
She was among the thin women
celebrating America's founding
and she waved the friendliest pale hand
and smiled the warmest faint smile.
I never saw her again.
I don't remember her name when sober.
I don't remember it when drunk.
It's like the many names
I remember then don't remember
from rock and roll to punk.
She was a young American woman.
We'd had a one-night stand,
many North Beach years ago.
No more Vietnams.

CRANE

How did the crane
get all the way on top
of that new building?

It didn't.
It was there to begin with.

The workers
built the building
like a nest
under the crane.

NY, NY

It's big
It's ugly
I hate it
I love it
I'm free
O
Talk to me
Can't you hear me
I can't leave it
I'll do anything for it
It's so big
It's filthy
It's so sweet
I adore it
I'm staying
I'll never leave
It's in me
It's so cruel
I hate it
I love it
It's mine
I own it
It's mine
Again and again
I say I hate war
I love it
It's disgusting
It's awesome
I love it
I won't go
I promise
It's beautiful
Talk to me
Can't you hear
Me loving

O it's so brutal
It's so shit
Talk to me
Tell me
What I should do
Anything
It's marvelous
I'll never stop
Loving it
Never never
Never never
Never

SWEATING BULLETS

And they said, Cuttheshit, we can talk faster
than a mind can read Marx, what's
all this commie bullcrap?

And they said, Avantgard and LSD.

And at the bottom of their argument
they said, Isn't St. Patrick's Cathedral
the grandest.

So naturally they all watch teevee
waiting for Lech Walesa
to get down on his knees
and kiss the Pope's hand.

And naturally they don't mind
that after the Pope leaves Nicaragua,
waves of contras pour in.
If only the same in Poland, they dream,

the millions of racist runaways
pouring into the city every day
from the suburbs

to make the doomed dollars move
while they sweat bullets,
they say, of peace.

STREETUNE

It was just
one of those

thongs.
So what?
It's the way

we do it, so
viet.

It's the way
we water
the flowers

in the garden
of spuds,
yes, spuds.

A street
that stands
around
fiery ashcans
in the winter.

A people
the dirty work
of god,
in this here America

the land of the
hah,

the home of the
bah,

year after year,
day after day,
the incredible
lies.

No wonder
the only good
drink is
Albanian
raki.

And no one can
get it,
and that's why
we organize.

SALT POINT

(A Socialist Realist Poem)

I was reading of the Albanian partisans
in Dritero Agolli's *Bronze Bust*
on a bus en route to a party
at the home of an old friend,
how Memo Kovaci planted
the first red seeds of cells
in the highland snow,
how the Lightning Battalion
chased the bestial Nazis.
At Market Street in San Francisco
I made my transfer walk
passing a small child selling
garlic blossoms at the gutter's edge,
a black woman playing music
for coins dropped into her guitar case,
two Indians with drunken crazed eyes
as if still unable to fathom
the land ripped out of their faces
to make strong cheekboned skyscrapers
and sleek-chinned cars.
Among the cable-car tourists there were
workers and the sullen unemployed
like dark or black Italians
milling around but with little to say,
and here and there
a man setting cardboard down
in a doorway,
or bending over,
or slowly toppling over from weariness
under the dusky sky, rag-blue
as an overcoat.

I kept reading of the Albanian greatness
on the transfer bus, thinking
how marvelous that genre
of peasant and red novels
which passes such living earth
to the imagination,
how such salt still could be tasted
and the struggle understood in all
its simplicity, under the platinum
sheen of cities and the immense
industrial complexity in which we lived.
It was a salt-point 'round which
my father raged all his life
and my mother was stillness for;
it was the salt-point for lack of which
my son had died and my daughter
struggled amid false images to remember.

Memo Kovaci was as real to me
as my closest comrade.

I entered the party
but the wall of grass flung me back
and the puppets of false liberty
made me sicken and loathe.
My old friend passed me in bodiless greeting
and I saw:
these men and women, activists of anarchy,
did what they could, mouthed
what the hot moment or the cold strings
insisted they mouthe.

They were free, given hell.
I was slave to their liberty.

But when I lowered my eyes
in the corner of that amplified room,
at the end of everything
that was memorable meaning,

I was walking with Memo Kovaci
through the snow.

WORDS ON THE WING

"She left the baby by the open window
where the dirty aprons go"
are lines we heard a woman say
as we were walking home.
You said they'd make
a great blues song
so it being Monday morn
I took the clothespins
to the lines,
hung them there like notes
to jive the baby by the open
window where the dirty aprons go.

OLD BLACK SHOE SONG

Two nights ago
I saw an old black shoe
alone on the sidewalk.
Last night
it was in the gutter.
I was feeling blue.
I was feeling small.
I hadn't seen you
for oh so long.
Now old black shoe's got me.
Put up a sail.
Floating down the gutter
in my exile.
Hope when I get there
you won't turn me down.
Can't go back to
where I come from.

IS

It is what I know of you,
the blues I sing,
the fragrance of the datura
you popped into my jacket pocket,
our living human or inhuman
smells together,
the tender youth of your breast,
the way your slight body
accepts a desperate centaur,
accepts, accepts, accepts.
Love in the umbra.
Love among the crippled and bent,
among trucks loaded with
Chinatown pigmeat,
love that mixes its dark seed
with the incompleted
blond yesterdays of tomorrows.
O wine of hungry midnights
and underneath our cries, our griefs,
the joy that just having to brings:
the necessary Is.

A GRAIN OF RICE

At the lip
of a garbage can
against a Chinatown wall
so small
and hunchbacked
she, or could it be he?
no, it's she, this International
Women's Day,
shining the rotten cheek
of an orange fished out
with a piece of the *Chinese Sun*.

What do I know
of black stockings
on the white thighs
of leisure imagination?

Molly's a lump of coal.
Sarah's a broccoli flower.
The hunchback a grain of rice
when I think of her again.
A grain of rice. A grain of rice
the world has eaten and eaten.
And still she grows and multiplies,
nourishes the centers even of blind eyes,
shines the world up with a smile
and the rotten things in cans.

REMEMBER!

Do you weep suddenly, unexpectedly
weep, or alone, sometimes, groan
huge as the child on the tracks
the size of the world's head
of Siquieros?

O nape of Grenada heeled by the boot
of Washington,
O Azania jailed by the uranium
and gold fingers of Johannesburg
and Washington.
One after another, daily, nation
after nation piled up inside us
like bodies in the crematorium
of Washington.
Remember!

THE CHAIN

Talk about your body of Doda,
talk about your kabbalah stone,
tell me did you ever hear
of a man called Dennis Goldberg?

If you go to Pretoria prison
he'll come out to meet you
on a chain.
Nineteen years old the chain.
Nineteen years solitary,
forced food.
Fifty year-old Goldberg
of the militant wing
of the African National Congress
against apartheid
and the like.

Talk about your sexual mysticism,
talk about your bigbang bribe
O imperialism
Wathint abafazi
Wathint imbokodo
Uzakufa
"you have struck a rock,
you have dislodged a boulder,
you will die."

A PRICELESS RADIANCE

What did they want, most of all,
on August 14, 1521, the Spaniards,
the first day after the fall
of Tenochtitlan, severed limbs
in the streets, gullies heaped
with corpses, the water blood,
undrinkable blood, the adobe
bloodied, the Aztec quetzal
feathers burned, the people
eating worms, what did they
want, the gods in quotes
who came on the mountains
floating on the water?

The same thing the contras
want, and their mercenary
allies, and their lackeys today
in Nicaragua, from the same
Nahuatl earth of a free people,
they want the gold, they will say
and do anything
to get the gold
but Sandinist Nicaragua
has already alchemized.
It is in the people now.
It is the people now.
A poor gold worth little
on the market of greed,
but for the people
of the world,
a priceless radiance.

THE LITERACY OF NICARAGUA

Before I ever arrived in Nicaragua
your revolution had planted
itself in my eyes.
Upon a hill in San Francisco
or in the streets where
blood is changed into
walking music, Nicaragua
already was more
than a name for its own sake.

My pen could feel the first
lessons of literacy
stammering up the ladders
alchemized from the deepwood bones
of your revolutionary heroes:
golden ladders of sound
because a people had torn
the chains from its neck
so that its phoenix earth
fly freely everywhere
like a construction
of tomorrows in poetry
and resistance
to the vampires gathering
with even more vicious fangs.

Now a man or woman or child
could put a fingertip
under the first syllable
of a poem by Ruben Darío
and continue to the end:
to the tenderness
of sound, heartbeat and idea
all in a single sigh.
Now a man or woman or child

43

could stroke the word
Esquipul
and the giant burnt corn,
the black Christ of the Great Bear,
the sun of the dark body of night
would glow in the umbra.
And Xilomena, the corn-goddess,
whose kernels
are all the *teotes*
since Xipe-totec,
and all the *otls*
and *umbas*
and *ziztlis*
would rise with the tumbling
of the moon down the slope
of the volcano of clouds
simply because
one could read what was written
and write what was spoken
by the stars through the branches
of the rivers.

Look, see there! he is painted
on the cranium of the sky
in the form of a hieroglyph:
Sandino, the constellation of the Exorciser.
And beside him, Carlos Fonseca,
the constellation of the Engineer of Resonances.
And there, where that cluster glows,
shifting and permutating, –
the Junta of the Construction of Rebirth.
For everything in our clench
now bears evidence
to the harvest of the new
seeds of a new sky.
And what is above
truly is what is below.

44

The sky no longer is a desperate
and superstitious escape.
It is the roof of the mouth
of a kid who fired a gun
against the Somocistas
before he could write his name
or the name of the tree
he leaned against
or the name of the mask he wore.
I remember him from the farmboy
thicket of New England's
Green Mountain Boys.
I remember him with the musket
and the handmedown rifle
of Loyalist Spain.
In the belly of the moon-mother
resisting Sinacan, he
was with Mujo Ulkinaku
on an Albanian turret
above the fascist armada,
or with Hector Riobé
in a cave the size of the groan
of all Haiti
against the terrors of the Macoutes.

Where I am from, the word
is continually poisoned
by the arsenic of the dollar.
A poem is a consolation
for the stuffing of the veins
of the rivers of the arms
with heroin.
A poem is a shamble of rooms.
Insanity in the eyes.
Pity which never is naked need
but laced with the violence

45

of want want want.
Where I am from, a poem
is an isolation desperate
for land,
a unity of destructions and sorrows,
a variation of slave-cries
freed to the choiceless bondage
of rackets and computerized minstrel shows.
Or else it's a magnificent
work of art which means
nothing because it serves
everything decayed and deranged
by profits – and so
its magnificence becomes
the shuck and hustle of critics
and neutral hacks.
And these fluent, poisoned rivers,
though they've never not known
education,
are more illiterate
than the four year-old
Nicaraguan entering
a wooden room to read.

I want to develop this theme,
that the guerrilleros and guerrilleras
are from thickets and streetcorners
we have known, that the sandinistas
are ourselves
arrived in a time
when the internationale is born
on the lips of national anthems,
and that it is Washington D.C.
which vampirizes in order
not to recognize itself
and would as soon throw the hood
of the KKK over the Empire State Building

46

rather than admit
that a Nicaragua
or a Vietnam
is actually its own
revolutionary resonance
passed through the heart-transplant
of Soviet Russia,
the agrarian incarnation
of Red China,
the birth of American brotherhood
of nearby Cuba,
and that such is
the real migration
of revolutionary earth.

MADE IN HAITI

Made in Haiti,
the ball
so much depends upon,
by a poor black woman
who earns $2.60 a day
for making a dozen of them,
a woman like the pregnant worker
shot by Duvalier goons,
or the ones spray-shot
for protesting her death in Gonaives,
where all other parties but Duvalier's
have been outlawed.

Forty thousand in a stadium here
(the whole population of Gonaives)
cheer the movement of the little ball
with *Made in Haiti* on it.
Inside it,
the sisal is packed like:
a population in prison,
a hungry weeping that literally
beggars the imagination,
and a core of revolutionary struggle
that will burst imperialism's stitches
and make that island
fair as its wondrous people.

HAITI

One day in the future these sounds are seeds of,
there will be a moment when not even the monkeys chirp in the
    trees,
when burros will hold their brays,
when the coconut-milky clouds will not stir in the sky,
when the thatchwork of huts will not be gossiping
and there is no breeze or sweat between your body and your rags
One day when that moment lived for years, for centuries, is here
and everything is still
like death
or zombie bread holding its breath,
a drum will begin sounding
and then another and another, multiplying,
and the voices of the simidors will be heard in every field.
And the backs,
those backs with everything written on them,
which have bent like nails hammered into the wooden cross
of the land for ages,
will plunge their arms into the ground
and pull out the weapons they've planted.
For the drums aren't an invitation to a voodoo ceremony.
The voices of the simidors are singing another song.
The lambis are growling lions of Africa.
And it isn't the cranium of a horse hung on the wooden cross
braided with limes;
it isn't a wooden cross at all that's planted in the good earth
of new Haiti.

On the night of that day the taste of a mango will be
a rapturous fireworks bursting and dying into
the ecstasy of the simple truth in our mouths.
Our acres will sleep with their arms round each other.
The child freed from terror and death will bound with
the boundless, and the maize amaze the sky upon waking
for as long as humanity is.

EL SALVADOR

"They would slit open
the stomach of a pregnant
woman and take the child out
as if they were taking
eggs out of an iguana."

And still Washington
anoints the head
of the junta with millions.

"They put a gun up her anus.
They found her head
somewhere else."

O unction of Reaganism
still pouring on the
murderer's heads.

"A dog was carrying
a newborn infant
in its mouth."

"In some stomachs
they put soap and coffee
as a mocking."

And still the money
rains down
into helicopters,
changes into bullets,
pours into the
thickets.

Our pockets
filled with blood.

50

AFTER CONGRESS

Slime senate,
thugs paid by robot caesars,
pepsodent smile speefreech doubletalkers
designed to kill poor farmers
and their families –
representatives of nothing
but supersonically decayed
corporate terrorists
terrified and crying terrorist –
your vote for war is but a moment,
your constituency is not
a bald eagle paperweight
but human hair
that will go on burning
long after you are finished.

THE SAFE

The safe!
The safe behind closed doors
or in the ivory towers of art
rather than culture!
The safe nicely banked!
The multinational safe
dispensing international money,
hush money,
babble-away-its-already-unheard
hush money.
Hush your mouth, honey.
The verse,
the universe,
the universal versateller
out in space
open 24 munitions hours a day:
that's the chip off the old blockhead
earth.
Some bargain!
Some deal!

THE TURKEY EATEN

The turkey eaten,
now the vast mass of money
pours into the streets, the dollar
moves through Union Square
with the rapidity of a New York
taxicab, the stockmarket rises
18 points; the Empire begins
its gift-bearing spree, people
in the San Francisco streets
might as well be in NY,
a chipper impersonality mingles
with the quickness of friendliness,
it is this time of year that 40%
of all the profits are made;
a Santa Claus walks the streets
passing out balloons and advertisements,
you can almost hear *jesus christ* on
the huffing and puffing along,
the newly-elected president
smiles in his White House
as if the buying were an offering
to his inauguration; never
has the nation been so wealthy,
so poor, so giving, so greedy, so clear,
so rotten, so free, so sheet-wrapped,
so impotent, so fucked, so burning.

THIS I KNOW

This I know:
the Demos
are nothing but the hustler
side of the Reps,
they're Siamese twins of profits
and always have been
and always will be.
And anyone fooled by them
is a damn fool.
Not just a fool,
but I mean a damn fool
like the shadow of
a parking meter
standing around in one place
waiting for the sun to come up.

JIVA

Our Indian friend
and comrade, Som,
what a fine feather!
So light of speech
and with so little
on his stomach.
In days of hunger,
I think of him
the way I do
of famished guerrilleros
in the thicket
of El Salvador,
or breaths that go on
breathing in mexican
rubble.
O indomitable umbilicals.
Tied to the roots of glory.

GUATEMALA

Through ten Greek women
poets in an anthology
the 10 beheaded heads
of 10 Guatemalan women
are speaking
a black and magnificent
rage that scratches
at the eyes of junta
and tears the bloody shrouds
into red flags
raised above the hovels
of their dying.

And if it is so, and it is so,
that the 10 year-old
Miskito indian prostitute
in Honduras
is the grand-daughter
of the first lady of the
United States,
a wave will rise in Lebanon,
a true cedar,
and wear leaves
of beheaded heads
and have branches
of innocent little bodies,

and fall nowhere but
against the White House
of the panderess.

THE BOTTOM LINE

The bottom line
is a bone bleached white
by the desert sun
a skewer meat once hung from
a hyphen of hunger
the zero parallel of world famine
the bottom line
is that white bone gnawed
by the maggots of the belly
of the dune
the bottom line
is a cup of hands
for years collecting drops of water
from the sky
O remember, you of the glutted
here and now,
those with neither,
those not yet and already so ancient,
if there is a literal and specific
it is them,
for you know, as I, that
our hungers and wants
are as the nothing of nothingness
compared to the empty
ragblown generations of their
staggering.

57

THIS NERUDA EARTH

Sitting against a treetrunk in Dolores Park
amid the Chilean solidarity gathering,
my eyes beheld three tiny daisies
in the grass, their little pollen hearts
attacked by flies. Nearby, yellowjackets
were flying over a jungle of blades
of grass and brilliantly green-backed
horseflies were making merry on
a flute of dogshit. I had lowered
my eyes from the speeches, and even
the People's Tribune was stacked at
my side. So much movement
in nature. A butterfly alighted on
the front page and walked along
the headline as if reading it. The
flies went on eating the hearts out.
The horseflies were absolutely drunken
on the excrement. The yellowjackets
were strafing and landing and
taking off again. It was the guerrilla
war, it was *mir,* it was peace. So much
movement, so much space in an inch. This
Neruda earth.

SPIRALS

Onward and upward,
the smoke from the chimneys
spirals,

spirals even today.
A generation and more
of clouds
made of Communists, Catholics,
Jews, Gypsies, Witnesses,
Gays.

Jet planes fly through
them. They
are all over the world,

rising and developing
joined with the burned
of El Salvador, the Hiroshima scorched,
the roasted starving
of Africa,
the diaspora
of Palestine in flames.

You smoke them, your
toke is them, we
blow the dead
away into air.

A black man
is tied to a tree
in Georgia and burned
to ash. 1893.
It spirals even today.

You will never
escape them,
they
arise
and develop,
invincibly.
Deny them
and try breathing.

They will haunt
you to the end
of your
sperm and your
egg.

In the
last
gasp
of the
molecule
they'll
arise.

"DEAD ANY OLD HOW"
– Jean Genet

"Dead any old how"
in a clutter of skinny bodies,
bloated black heads
the elbow narrow alleys
of Sabra and Shatila themselves.

The flies hiving at a dead groin
or scissored fingers.
They sink in, I chew
on a bone of garlic
to clean the poison
out of me, the mass
graves we've become

since Jonestown
Palestine
Grenada.

A rag of a tent blows in the breeze.
No, it is the skirt and sash
of the old woman Homeland
killed over and over.

It is the flag of migration
flapping its wings
after the fact.

His eyes are made of rubble
on Rubble Hill. In the cracks
an invincible light is dawning.

61

THE WRITING ON THE WALL

A delicate wisp of
palestinian arabic ink

makes all the kabbalas
think and rethink.

A whirling turban
on a dancer's head

resurrects the Lebanese dead.
The weight of vengeance slips

on its own armored obesity.
A kid leaps from rubble to rubble

announcing the revolutionary
dawn.

THE CRIME

The crime wasn't in the subway
but up above
in the stock exchange
in the skyscrapers
and the banks stuffed with human sweat
converted into bullion,
and that's what the vigilante was protecting
and what the grand jury exonerated him for,
because – and the ghettos and jammed prisons
will attest to the fact these days –
at the heart of the big buck is an apartheid
no fucking different than South Africa's.

HOMAGE TO BEN MOLOISE, SOUTH AFRICAN POET

When a poet
in revolutionary struggle
is hanged by the evil his every breath had fought
his words
unleash the lynched
unchain the fettered
turn every pen into a javelin
when a poet
is murdered for being
truth's messenger
the government of his executioners
chokes on its own tongue
and aparthate crawls on maggot belly
while the words of the poet
enter the peoples' ears
like the unbroken neck of the rainbow
that will be South Africa's sky
for every pair of eyes
when the reign of death is over
and the flood subsides.

UNDERGROUND

So clearly that the primary vowels
are understood
and the consonants are consonant
and this is a very deep wisdom
now it is in you
and you must carry it
as one carries a child.
For the moment never mind our rage
which is an elision on our age,
which is a vintage and a grape.
See the staves splashed with blood
see the blood torqued with atonality –
time is, and so we become
what can be wrought or plumbed
or bent or straightened,
we play the sick and passive
bedridden verbs
with a moment gainsaid
with eyes like windows blown out
by random explosions;
we are the crutches under armpits
and the hospitals of inches,
we are soupcans in trembling hands
and the small change of a spring
night in the America of sorrows,
we sound like jews because
we are palestinians,
we die and catch our breath,
we somersault with struggle;
everything bought and commodified
throws itself at the edge of our pages
like a knife to cut us open,
to read us at the table of oil;
but we refuse the operation,
we proliferate our secret leaves

underground for that is our name,
underground for that is the key
to the movement that wears
life as a mask
and death as a trust of memory
blossoming with children
on the thigh of every nation's hill.

ATHEIST

To say Passover is absurd after
the egyptological ellipsis
of Israel itself,
and that Easter's a lie after
the palmsunday acquittal
of the Greensboro gang
is not to opt for the Buddha's
popsicle moment
or Islam's demagoguery
of satin oil.
They *all* want you to wear
blinders to the international
human race, which
"challenges divinity
with a smile."
Leninism levels.

THAT'S ALL

Sitting on the grass with Sarah.
Danny Kim came over and sat down
with his lonely football.
He spoke of the grass, how it
wasn't the best, "hard
grass," he said, though it seemed
to me not unlike an English
meadow. Then he talked
of Buddha and incarnation,
his hand vaguely pointing
over there – to a tree?
or space? For some moments
my mouth fell open
and the same kind of confusion
overcame me, that I used
to see in David when he
didn't altogether understand,
and for those few moments
I was my dead son absolutely.
That's all.

EZRA DOG

I

Did you say Ezra
            Dog?
I did.
Do you mean Ezra, the dog of the beautiful
filipino woman who lives on the Beach?
I do not. I mean Ezra Dog
Pound. And his kennel
of little whelps.
Who bark about what a great poet
Ezra Dog was, and is,
even though his politics was bad,
who apologize for his wet black
boughs to the gunmen of Europe,
for his wet black bowwows
while patrols sweep wetbacks
into the corrals of Texas,
stuff them into trucks
the way the gunmen did the jews
while Ezra Dog down the road
was whining on Italian
radio about the halfbreeds of Europe,
about the gorillas of America,
those jews, and those blacks
being lynched by plantation folk
with pitches of voice in the crux
no different than dead dog Ezra's.
And now that Ezra's republican
eco eco economic
fascism's written on everybody's brow,
and that sell-out's liberty
and the sell-out liberties
of this yipyip-hooray American
experiment

69

has the universities of the nation
churning out those wagtag
little foams and grovels of capitalism,
and even the broad lap
of the Zionism he denounced,
in sadistic benignity
with Buddha, Confucius, and Tao (Jones)
lets his image lie across it
like a mongrel pieta,

I'm goin' down to the dock
and see that Dog, the shepherd of Germany
gets the hell out of San Francisco and
back to South Africa
with its cargo of rabies.

II

And, and I use the word
advisedly,
when Dog was kenneled in St. Elizabeth's,
defended by literateurs
and young snipperwhaps
in rebellion against the family
grey matter of desolation
after the Bomb,
"in Italy" he told Charles Olson,
"I was always a Stalinite,
never a Trotskyist."

Can you beat that
mutt?!

Who'd barked against bolsheviks
throughout the thirties and forties,
whose cantos are

usury's imperialist
invasion of arrogance's images
on workingclass senses,
and who would take up
with the racist John Casper,
even while in the sickhouse
and scribble jingo gibberish
for his southern hatesheet.

All the while being apologized for
by cold-war saps of technique,
honored by Bollingen
stuffed stiffs,
even proto-beatniks,
for his contribution to American letters,
his breaking of new ground,
his imagistic elegance,
his translative prowess.
In the new age of power through
schizophrenia,
in the loose corners of the mouth
of marijuana,
in the new cycle, the immigration
of the corporate state,
the fascist's sell-out experimentalism
would be evoked and re-evoked
until, lo and behold,
universities and writing cliques
were glutted
with Dog's disciples:
packs of America's finest
writing hounds
all pardoned,
like himself,
for writing well,
according to the book (the bankbook)
by the hicks of hell.

J. my name is Jack
and my woman's name is Sarah.
We come from San Francisco
and we don't sell the people.

IT – STARES

The Cherokees' first word
for car was: ditulena,
it – stares.

How faraway Soweto is
in indifferent eyes!
But Soweto is tomorrow!

WATCH OUT FOR THE SPIRIT VENDORS

Who shuts the gates to the mouth?
The spirit vendors.
Who are the spirit vendors?
Just what it says.
Get your spirit, get your free spirit
only it isn't free.
Get your big glass of hotel
while the pickets pretzel outside.
Get your big baseball stadium
with a price on every hide.
Spirit vendors everywhere around:
looked under a newspaper,
walked on a demo line,
couldn't not feel spirit vendors
at every turn
ready to price the spirit
in ounces and pounds;
wrap it in neon, ribbon it
with rock, keep the people
bought and sold like
supersonic schlock.
Spirit vendors on the loose
with plenty bux to spend.
Raise the level
of nothing to the enth.
Couple of trees were talking
this morning in the park,
couple of natural stems,
couple of physical barks.
How long before
we're price-tagged,
one said to the other.
Spirit vendor came along
and said to the tree:
you mother!

74

And put a price called
Dispensable on its beautiful
form.
Watch out for spirit vendors
if you still remember mom.

A FLEA'S KNEES

A flea's
knees
not a flea's
feet
is where
a flea jumps from.
I heard it
on the radio
on one
of those
Smithso-
nian Institute
shows
where they
have
fleas on
their knees.
Workers,
watch out
for whom
Hormel tolls.
It tolls for
fleas
on their knees.
Stand tall
all over the land.
Dump those
scabs and
lousy bosses
for liberty.

DREAD-BLOODED AMERICAN

To perpetuate:
but what is troubling now?

I don't see, I don't hear, I don't feel
anything

yet eat this peach, listen to a poem, fuck
and cry 'I love you' in the depth

of the gyzym of soul;
yet have this sense

I don't see, I don't hear, I don't feel,
anything.

This is a political contradiction.
It is a dying more dying than dead,

this united states of
get-lost from the inside-out,

this always Away, even
in the closest embrace,

yet nowhere to go which
isn't or wouldn't be anything else

under any other circumstances
for a thousand years

than money, rich money,
reich money,

upon which this sleazy independence
depends.

THING-COMMODITY

The spirit doesn't move very far
before: Thing.
Thing-commodity everywhere
including our bodily relations now.
Where, outside dumb safe heavens of schools
or chiseling fames, do words
blunder and stumble, groan like at birth,
moan like at death?
Even the young are patsies
wired to the general hopheadtunism
of the musical buck's
"perennial fashion":
survival going round and round
in the earphone isolation
of walking control rooms.
You were saying something about a woman friend.
I looked out of the bus window
on Mission St.
A pile-up at the sewer mouth.
Clenched cans
of Budweiser and Pepsi,
plastic cups, a plastic-covered
milkshake cup stabbed
with a straw, balls of paper,
a cigaret pack, a piece of rag,
the specific debris of the street.
But the rainwater swirling
through them into the grate
was torrential in miniature.
Riverrapids, oceans
in a flash. Flashflood,
lightningstroke,
the concrete universe
of energy that made
the dead debris monumental,

78

the sewer a giant reservoir.
The stoplight mine.
The half-minute my very own.
I'll remember this through everything
and write of it tomorrow,
I told myself.
"She didn't mean it that way," I said
as the bus continued on.

DARK MONDAY

Listening to Billie
Holiday
I told the waitress
she was getting
better every year.

On the ground in a rainy
doorway
downtown:
the tiny brown tits
of a throwaway
cupcakes container.

Dark Monday
dark money
way down yonder
in the pockets
of your jeans.
Bessie spits:
"Don't gimme that
good morning shit,"
smiling
at the Monday
cash
register machine.

1953

What has character
downtown amid the professional
buildings, the highrise
glass buildings,
is the one in the state
of being demolished,
its guts hanging
out of the broken stories,
flashes of the original
red beams observable
amid the gaping
holocaust of gravel
and broken walls,
a naked shambles
a generation or two old
strangely intimate
and even familiar
like an argument
about whether
or not socialism
can ever get started
in america
between
a father and son
in 1953.

DEEP MEMORY I

The weathered wood
on the floor
of the pony cart
I rode around the block
in as a child
came to me
just before sleep
almost half
a hundred years ago
last night.

DEEP MEMORY II

I dreamed today at the edge of waking beside you
a dark girl at whom I threw kiss after kiss
but she lay dead beyond my feeling,
and that was just, as I woke beside you

whom I love by light and night.
That other is dead and not.
My kisses, I see, were tears
for one of the forms dreams take

of my long gone brother.

DEEP MEMORY III

Looking up
from writing Agim Gjakova
in Tirana,
the smell of my father's mother's
topfloor slum dwelling
in the Bronx
– uncomfortable to many,
unbearable to many,
perfectly at home
to me –
wrapped me
in generations of realism
I struggle to make socialist
with these olfactory sensings
of the New
Year 1985.

THE COCKROACH

When I returned to my room
a roach was floating
in the remains
of my glass of straight vodka.
A cockroach, poor thing.
But the way to go these days
when we carry bags, or cameras
or earphones or red papers
and are still stripped of everything
but a drop of love
and even that half-mocks us
in some of the most beautiful
faces sucking cock
on the covers of porno magazines.
I ran into your girlfriend in the park.
We sat and fed breadcrumbs
to the birds. Among the pigeons
there was the tiniest sparrow,
its beak wide open, squawking
squawking for no reason at all
for even after it pecked up
a good sized piece, it wanted
to squawk and couldn't squawk
and eat at the same time
and so it finally flew away
with the bread. And the madwoman
who all winter and spring has
strutted and cardboard-bedded
and junk-collected in the park,
talking to no one but her demons
– even she is small changing now.
A miracle! The poverty they feed us
can drive even the insane sane.
Her head a fist all season
shaking at herself

opens like a hand
and jerks the coins up to her eyes
because at least,
to say the least,
she still counts.

Poor thing, you did as well
until you fell into
this well of vodka.
Well, at least your
crawl is over, as we say.
The way to go these days
of dole and guzzle
and friends like islands
without a song.
Life is short, the draining long.

HOW SHOCKING

How shocking the total
nakedness
of the woman in the glass
case of pornography
who though
usually harnessed in the corner
of my passing eye
appeared
to have taken off
all her clothes
and for a moment
stood huge
(though she was slight)
and free
(though in slavery)
like the clear thought
of the class struggle
just before she
had to slip back into
another price.

SQUATTERS

Doorways I have passed:
the open palms,
the displaced hair,
the wayward resignation
of an abbreviated brother,
hey, bro.
can you . . . ?
lemme have a?
and what woman laughs
a real live round bouncing
baby belly laughter
anymore?
Everyone knows it's the government
that really practices abortion.

The red flag
blowing in the breeze,
the flag with holes in it
like the eyes of escaped zombies,
the flag old as earthquakes
riddled with cracks
of face.
In its furl the squatters
find allegiance.
Obsolete knotholes of a poor
ballgame still breathing.
The wooden planks
of primal beds.
The chips of walls that still
defy the sickness
of skyscraper hospitals.
The fugitive neighborhood.

Into the abandoned silos,
those busted clarinets of cities,

they come with hammer
and sickle, wrench
and nails;
in Frisco, Azania, France,
Amsterdam
the homeless army
drives a wedge
of struggle and resistance
that makes the wood
stand fast with them
and the air throw
a skin of flame
around their
music. There is a peal
of thunder graffiti
written on the army's
left flank:
We will not be suicided by skyscrapers!
The hole in the wall is a secret
panel!
The underground candle glows!

HOME

(for the National Union of the Homeless)

Winter has come.
In doorways, in alleys, at the top
of churchsteps,
under cardboard, under rag-blankets
or, if lucky, in plastic sacks,
after another day of humiliation,
sleeping, freezing,
isolated, divided, penniless,
jobless, wheezing, dirty
skin wrapped around cold bones,
that's us, that's us in the USA,
hard concrete, cold pillow,
where fire? where drink?
damned stiffs in a drawer
soon if, and who cares?
shudders so familiar to us,
shivers so intimate, our hands finally closed in clench
after another day panhandling, tongues
hanging out;
dogs ate more today, are curled
at the feet of beds, can belch, fart,
have hospitals they can be taken to,
they'll come out of houses and sniff
us dead one day,
pieces of shit lying scattered here
in an American city
renowned for its food and culture.

The concrete is our sweat hardened,
the bridge our vampirized blood;
the downtown, Tenderloin and Broadway
        lights — our corpuscles transformed into ads:
our pulse-beat the sound *tengtengenteng*

of coins piling up on counters, in
phonebooths, Bart machines, *tengtengenteng*
in parking meters, pinball contraptions,
public lavatories, toll booths;
our skin converted into dollar bills,
plastic cards, banknotes, lampshades
for executive offices, newspapers, toiletpaper;
our heart — the bloody organ the State
gobbles like a geek in a sideshow
that's become a national circus of the damned.

O murderous sytem of munitions and inhuman rights
that has plundered our pockets and dignity,
O enterprise of crime that calls us criminals,
terrorism that cries we are fearful,
greed that evicts us from places we ourselves have built
miserable war-mongery that sentences us to misery
        and public exposure as public nuisances to
        keep a filthy republic clean —
this time we shall not be disappeared
        in innercity ghetto barrio or morgue,
this time our numbers are growing into battalions
        of united cries:

We want the empty offices collecting dust!
We want the movie houses from midnite til dawn!
We want the the churches opened 24 gods a day!
We built them. They're ours. We want them!
No more doorways, garbage-pail alleys,
no more automobile graveyards,
underground sewer slums.
We want public housing!
No more rat-pit tubing, burnt-out rubble-caves,
no more rain-soaked dirt in the mouth,
empty dumpster nightmares of avalanches of trash
        and broken bricks,
screams of women hallucinating at Muni entrance gates,

no more kids with death-rattling teeth under discarded tarp.
We want public housing!
we the veterans of your insane wars,
workers battered into jobless oblivion,
the factory young: fingers crushed into handout
          on Chumpchange St.,
the factory old: spat-out phlegm from the sick
          corporate chest of profits.
Instead of raped respect, jobs
with enough to live on!
Instead of exile and eviction in this,
our home, our land,
Homeland once and for all
for one and all
and not just this one-legged cry
on a crutch on a rainy sidewalk.

KIDSKIN

That feeling – all day almost
entirely falling asleep
inside some fallopial
dream or skin of skins –
of women
workers yearning out
of the times of the wage,
that almost
kidskin or pointing to
the dark underumbra
of the movement of the
bux . . ."it's business," one
winged at my ear; "she's
got her jacket," another
said in passing; "that's
why I'm goin' to the
meat market" still
another said. The day
after I wrote my first
poem in Albanian,
it feels soft as a breast.

NIGHTSCAPE I

You see them
        round about
     midnight, in Chinatown
sidestreets or in doorways
        directly on Kearny
in the shadow of the great
    bat pyramid:
not simply dead drunk,
but as if dead, drunk,
on their backs sprawled,
open-mouthed
or on their faces, or
so beggarly in their wine,
they sit in doorways
asking change
from anything that moves:
a blown piece of newspaper,
the shadow of a pigeon
in the moonlight.

NIGHTSCAPE II

I wonder
did that stumplegged
wino lying on the sidewalk
last night between two
                crutches –

a couple of cops walked by him
without doing anything –

it's hot outside tonite, said
the porn queen on the cover
of the magazine in the glare of the light by the
Adult Bookstore's open door facing his sleeping eyes.

GARDENIA

That woman walking talking to herself
in furs.
And that one in the doorway smelling
of cardboard and rags, mumbling.
And that man, drunk, babbling on the sidewalk,
Chinese, holding a pink plastic bag.
And that man, sober, talking to a lampost,
and that young hooker, in front of the hotel,
smelling of dead orgasms,
venereal acne broken out on her face,
whispering to herself with a sullen
rat of lip:

dislocated, deranged, dissident, atonal,
joyless, loveless, timewarped,
space-killed,
eaten by the worms of money,
bitten-away faces, loneliness handouts,
pitiful claptrap dimes,

—over the ear of Socialism
they are petals of the most fragrant gardenia
and every single one of their syllables is heard.

THE BASKET

The basket, alone,
        in the rain
in the Chinatown
alley.
Torn bottom.
Two handles
good for
nothing.
Duck eggs!
Dried lizards for
emphysema.
Umbrella
hats pouring
along the sidewalk.
I stir some grey
sky in with my tea.
The leaves form
the busiest
intersection.
There we go
hand in hand
through a
downpour
of calligraphy.

THE SCISSORS

A second
            umbilical
must be cut
before one lives.
The first one brings
you into the world.
But the second
is formed of
the world itself
and yourself
twisted into
a hemp of blindness,
pulling you toward
capitulation,
negation
and the slavery
to decay.

Marxist-Leninism
is, among other
things, a scissors.

IRANCONTRASCAM

Worms, military worms defending their wormhood;
congressional worms squirming beneath the make-up
of the public farce; worms who, to a man,
crawled into power on tickets of greed and profits,
on mass graves and mutilated ditches —
the lid has been lifted by the still possible
kids of the world: yes, Americans, Nicaraguans,
Iranians, Palestinians, Haitians, Azanians, Koreans
have lifted it and now gaze with the rest
of uprising earth at the can of worms
still wriggling out its boring, malicious,
iniquitous and pompous drivel:

We're the freest!   (A lie
We're the most open!   (A lie
We're the most patriotic   (A lie
We're the most constitutional! (A lie
We're the most powerful   (A lie

What a sickening squidge of dirty viscous grey!
Let's put the lid back on it forever!
Let's seal it and pitch it into the ocean,
those mealy little screws of imperialism
that have caused such misery and suffering
and isolation on earth.
Let the titanic lies that they are sink to
the bottom, slimy, disgusting beyond all vomit.
An airtight finish.
A vacuum-packed end.
Let's spare even the fishes.

JUNETEENTH

In Kinopravda 21
last night we saw Lenin,
in one of Dziga
Vertov's cinematic songs,
superior to The Man
With the Movie Camera,
we actually saw Lenin
move, talk, inflame
the workers
on Juneteenth Night 1986,
the letters of the film text
gigantic on the screen
between images
of his life and death;
saw the starving and homeless;
saw the USSR fighting off
intervention on the Slovak front;
heard a voice in the theater
cry out: Long Live Dora Kaplan!
when the name of the woman
who'd wounded Lenin
was uttered on the screen;
cried back: Long Live Lenin!
on the actual anniversary
of the emancipation proclamation,
which had occurred one day
after the emancipation
of the Russian serfs – O
may the hungry and homeless
in my own native land, O
may those natives facing
relocation in their very own
sacred land, O may this
people of every form and color
tear off the subtly lowered

hoods of crime and klan
that capital has sewn,
and be its own face within,
stuff hunger
down the throats of the millionaires,
throw houses
out of the landlords' windows
and feel at last,
without some stupid chagrin,
the joy of: Long Live Lenin!

ONWARD AND UPWARD

A three year old girl
sitting on a sofa
held in her lap
a one year old boy
with a pacifier
in his mouth.
Continually she
kissed his cheeks,
first one then
the other,
very naturally,
as we strove
around them
to understand
why it is we
embrace what
is new and
fresh in its
onward and
upwardly
spiraling motion
and not the
already
solidified
and dying away.

THE UNITY

A violinbow
along the edge
of a diamond –
where Blok's 12
and Webern's *series*
meet,
Celan is still falling
through the China sky
from the bottom of the Seine.

These lines from
two days ago,
to be worked
and reworked
into the presence.
A tension of
the non-objective
everywhere, the death
by cocaine I read
the score on faces,
the "forget its"
the "son of a bitches" I hear,
resonances of nothing.
Splinters of the red-
wood, how to
sequoyah
the music of the Left
when all the leaves,
the abbreviations,
are at each others' bark
and agribusiness dogs.

To work this
to be reworked.
We are in the territory

103

of the CPUSA. A thread
of sorrow, a violinbow
of consolation
for the school of the suicided,
the sound that links
the classes
of this school, to make this
work, rework –
the manuscript is job
and all the daughters
from that last line
of Weldon Kees
to Guyana imbedded in the heart,
"Nobody but fools ever thought it
was an easy trade"
when she no longer comes
into focus, at the base
of the spine, when she has
said "nothing is"
and only the anarchy of the wind
and only the snow
under the eyelids, indistinguishable
from the flesh of parties split.

We are in the territory
of the RCP. Black
laughter of the tones
of the howl against, thrust
of the immediate
act
over the bones of the dead
alamos, we are all Damians
holding the red flag aloft, are
the music itself – vanguard
minds artless to reveal
land, not the skyteeming suicides,
no ma, Mao!

no music but what we have won
by presence, not
ausencia, religion, but
attack, counterattack:
for every baseball, a new
Haitian born;
for every sentence
the double exclamation of
liberty.

And you, five, quintet
who plays beyond the grave
the fiercest melody,
Greensboro. And we
in the territory of the CWP,
innumerable notes
from where many yet cannot
understand,
innumerable sounds occurring
at moments – cries,
protests of martyrdom,
justified dreadnaught,
the land sopping in your dying
wounds!
At point zero, where
the naked truth is flayed,
what brave tonalities
O work this, to be
reworked
into existence

опять песня
ибо теперь
мы в местности
СПЛ

и песня
восходит через
народ негритянский.
Здесь отечество—
песня,
голос дома
во рту
как солидарность
которой
нет конца

once again, the song
because now
we are in the territory
of the CLP

and song
rises across
the Negro Nation.
Here land
is song,
the voice at home
in the mouth
like the solidarity
for which
there is no ending